Innovation

JOHN BESSANT

London, New York, Munich,
Melbourne, and Delhi

Editor Daniel Mills
US Editor Margaret Parrish
Senior Art Editor Helen Spencer
Production Editor Ben Marcus
Production Controller Hema Gohil
Executive Managing Editor Adèle Hayward
Managing Art Editor Kat Mead
Art Director Peter Luff
Publisher Stephanie Jackson

DK DELHI
Editors Alka Ranjan, Ankush Saikia
Designer Malavika Talukder
Design Manager Arunesh Talapatra
DTP Designers Preetam Singh, Pushpak Tyagi

First American Edition, 2009

Published in the United States by DK Publishing
375 Hudson Street, New York, New York 10014

09 10 11 12 10 9 8 7 6 5 4 3 2 1

ND140—November 2009

Published in Great Britain by Dorling Kindersley Limited.

A catalog record for this book is available from
the Library of Congress.

ISBN 978-0-7566-5555-6

DK books are available at special
discounts when purchased in bulk for sales
promotions,premiums, fund-raising, or
educational use.For details, contact: DK
Publishing Special Markets, 375 Hudson
Street, New York, New York 10014 or
SpecialSales@dk.com.

Color reproduction by
Colorscan, Singapore
Printed in China by WKT

Discover more at **www.dk.com**

Contents

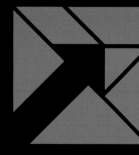

Introduction

In today's dynamic and turbulent world, organizations face a stark challenge—change or perish. Unless they keep renewing their products and services, and update the ways they create and deliver them, they risk being overtaken by competitors. Innovation—the process of change—is critical to the success of all organizations, large or small, in both the private and public sectors.

Most managers understand the importance of the topic. But making it happen requires a systematic, hands-on approach. We have to learn to manage innovation, and *Innovation* provides a framework for doing this. Key elements in successful leadership of innovation include developing a clear strategic vision and communicating it, searching for innovation triggers, choosing a balanced portfolio of projects, and delivering these projects on time and within budget.

Innovation is about human creativity, organized and applied across the organization. As a manager, you need to understand how the innovation process works and how you can mobilize this creativity. By using the guidelines and tools in this book, you will develop the skills you need to become an architect of change within your organization.

Chapter 1

Understanding innovation

Innovation is vital to the success of any business. But before you can apply it to your own organization, you need to understand what it is, why it is important, and how it applies to different business areas.

Tackling the basics

The word "innovation" today appears everywhere—on company websites, in advertisements for everything from hairspray to healthcare, on the lips of politicians, and in news features. However, while the word itself is popular, the concept of innovation remains poorly defined.

LOOK AT ALL AREAS
Human history shows that any area of life can benefit from innovation. Think about ways of improving even the most well-established systems in your organization.

Defining innovation

The word "innovation" comes from the Latin words *in* and *novare*, meaning "to make something new, to change." In principle, that's something anyone can do—imagination and creativity come as standard equipment for human beings. And it's something we've been doing since the earliest days when our ancestors lived in caves—the reason that we don't still live there is because of innovation. Working out better ways of hunting, mastering fire and tool-making, learning about agriculture, construction, transportation—quite simply, the history of civilization is about innovation.

Making innovation practical

There's still plenty of room for ideas to improve the world we live in—and we are still really good at coming up with them. But innovation isn't just about bright ideas; it's also about putting those ideas into practice. No matter how good the idea, it will not benefit your organization if it cannot be transformed into a practical change in the work process that increases efficiency or profit. A working definition of innovation would be: innovation = ideas + implementation.

TIP

KEEP AN OPEN MIND

Consider all ideas, no matter how strange, in their initial stages. Something that appears totally impractical at first may lead to useful thinking about other, more workable solutions.

Understanding the issues

Thinking about managing innovation raises three key issues. First, why should we innovate? Innovation always involves risks, and the rewards are not always obvious. Second, what can we change? You need to understand the options for innovation before you can make decisions on where to focus your efforts. And finally, how can we make it happen?

The innovation process

IDEAS
The starting point for innovation is an idea for improving an aspect of your operations.

＋

IMPLEMENTATION
Your idea must become a practical reality before it can benefit your organization.

＝

INNOVATION
Successful innovation takes place only when both of these elements are achieved.

Understanding the benefits

In Charles Darwin's famous theory of evolution, survival depends on an ability to change. Those species that do not adapt and change to cope with an altering environment simply die out. The same can be said to be true of business organizations as well.

Innovating to survive

If you do not change what you create and offer the world (your products and services), you run the risk of being pushed aside by organizations that do. And if you want your businesses to grow, you are unlikely to achieve this if you do not offer new products and services in new ways. This survival idea may be obvious in a competitive business world—but it is just as important in nonprofit organizations and public services.

ADDED COMPLEXITY
Offering something too complex for others to imitate places your product at a premium.

NOVELTY IN PROCESS
A faster, cheaper, or more efficient production process gives you an instant advantage.

RIGHT TIMING
Getting into a market early establishes your brand before the competition has time to develop.

Profiting from innovation

NEW COMPETITIVE FACTORS
Changing the base of your competition (eg, from price to quality) can undermine your rivals.

PROTECTING INTELLECTUAL PROPERTY
New trademarks and patents generate revenue through fees for their use.

PRODUCT OR SERVICE NOVELTY
Offering a product no one else has access to guarantees you will have no competition.

REWRITING THE RULES
Offering people something absolutely novel can create an entirely new market.

Innovating to make a profit

Innovation is essential to survival, and also to development and profit. There are many ways in which innovation can improve an organization's revenue and customer base, and defend against competitors. These range from making existing processes more efficient, to producing something before competitors can imitate it, to completely rewriting the rules of competition in your market.

Setting a pace for innovation

In order to manage the process of making innovations happen, it is important to understand the different ways in which change can be categorized. In this field it is not a case of "one size fits all"—you need to tailor your approach. One way is to look at how much "newness" is involved—from incremental small steps to radical leaps forward.

TIP

ENCOURAGE HIGH INVOLVEMENT
Everyone is creative—make sure you are tapping into this rich resource by asking employees for their ideas and suggestions to improve what your organization is trying to achieve.

Innovating in stages

The results of innovation can be dramatic—from the first-ever automobile to landing a man on the Moon. But many of these innovations come about not through dramatic changes but by doing the same things a little bit better. Incremental innovation—innovating in small steps—is about improving products and services and the processes we use to make them, making things better in quality and cheaper. Incremental innovation may not be glamorous and instantly noticeable, but it is by far the most common kind of innovation.

For example, most things you might buy in the supermarket are not "new to the world" products, but improvements and extensions of existing products. In service industries such as hotels and catering, innovation is about "doing what we do better"—improving the level and quality of service around a basic formula. In manufacturing, most innovation is about improving the way processes work—fixing bugs in the system, improving efficiency, quality, safety, and, importantly, reducing cost. This is not a one-time act, but the result of incremental improvement.

CASE STUDY

Incremental innovation
The French company, Bic introduced the Crystal ballpoint pen in 1951, and it is still going strong today. It's gone through all kinds of incremental improvement—in the ink formulation, in the ball point, in the plastic used, in the ways in which it is manufactured—but it is still the same old design. And it still does very well—sales are around 14 million pens per day. In 2002, Bic sold its 100 billionth pen—enough to cover 40 times the distance from Earth to the Moon, lined up end to end.

Innovating radically

Doing what we do better will get us a long way—but from time to time something comes along that changes the whole nature of a business or market, offering a great leap forward. This is known as radical innovation. Radical changes in products, services, and processes don't happen every day, and it takes a long time for them to be perfected, but they do have a big impact. Significant examples include electric power, cars and railroads, the Internet, and self-service shopping.

Managing innovation types

Understanding the difference between different types of innovation is important in learning how to manage it. Incremental innovation requires you to mobilize large numbers of people to make small improvements. The process is relatively low risk and high frequency, and forms part of the mainstream activity in most organizations. Radical innovation is much riskier and often takes specialized knowledge. It tends to be managed by dedicated teams, often outside the mainstream of the organization's workflow.

The development of most products tends to consist of long periods of incremental change punctuated with occasional radical breakthroughs. For example, the 20th century saw decades of incremental innovation of the standard filament light bulb to create smaller, more reliable, and more efficient versions of the original design. Now, however, light-emitting diodes (LEDs) promise a radical replacement in the form of a long-lasting and energy-efficient alternative. A successful organization should not limit itself to either incremental or radical innovation, but be prepared to engage in both, and manage them under the same roof.

HOW TO... BUILD AN INNOVATION PORTFOLIO

List all the possible innovations you could make.

↓

Arrange them by impact area: product, service, process, market.

↓

Score each idea in terms of impact and ease of implementation.

↓

Plot on a chart with impact and implementation on the two axes.

↓

Pick out easy to implement and high-impact ideas to work on first.

↓

Look at other high-impact ideas that may be harder to implement.

Directing innovation

In addition to incremental and radical changes, innovation can be defined by direction—by what is being changed. An organization can innovate its product, its process, its market position, or its business model. Together with incremental and radical innovation, these give an idea of your "innovation space" and help you decide where to innovate.

TIP

CONSIDER ALL OPTIONS

Keep reviewing the performance of your organization in all four directions, so you are always aware of the potential for innovation.

Products and processes

The most obvious areas of innovation are in what you produce and how you produce it. Product or service innovation can mean improving existing models—such as producing the latest CD player— or introducing something new—such as the first MP3 player. Process innovation can involve improving current processes—reducing waste, increasing efficiency—or changing the way you operate—such as switching from paper to digital correspondence.

The four innovation directions

CHANGING METHODS
The process—the way you create and deliver the product or service.

CHANGING WHAT IS OFFERED
The product or service— what you offer to the world.

Markets and models

Changing your business model and the market in which you operate may be more difficult, as they can affect the structure of your organization. However, they can prove extremely profitable: cell-phone makers at the turn of the century successfully transformed their product from a staid business tool into a mass-market fashion item with a strong youth market. Similarly, luxury car makers such as Rolls Royce, unable to compete on price with cheaper car producers, changed their business model to supply the trappings of a luxury lifestyle—vacations, watches, designer clothes—rather than simply a mode of transportation.

IN FOCUS...
OPEN INNOVATION

Innovation has always been a multiplayer game, involving weaving together technological, market, financial, legal, and other strands into creating new products, services, and processes. But in a world where markets are fragmented and globally spread, and global investments in R&D produce nearly $1 trillion of new knowledge every year, even the largest firms with big innovation budgets are increasingly aware of the importance of sharing knowledge. The idea of "open innovation"—originally the title of a book by US professor Henry Chesbrough—is that firms need to open up their innovation search and share their own knowledge.

CHANGING BUSINESS CONTEXT
The position—who you offer it to in the market and the story you tell about it.

CHANGING BUSINESS MODEL
The business model—the way you think about what your organization does and for whom.

Innovating successfully

Any innovation project involves a degree of risk—there is always the chance that it might fail. It is important for any organization undertaking innovation to be aware of the factors that make innovations more likely to succeed, and to be able to identify those that are likely to fail.

Identifying successful innovations

The history of product and process innovations is littered with examples of apparently good ideas that failed—in some cases with spectacular consequences. Most organizations would own up to having problems with making innovation happen, including a fair proportion of ideas that are never realized, and new initiatives that flop more or less embarrassingly. However, a great deal of research has gone into identifying the key areas on which organizations can focus to promote successful innovation. It might not be possible to guarantee success every time, but paying attention to the key aspects can stack the deck in your favor. Remember, innovation doesn't happen by accident, but by careful planning.

CASE STUDY

Long-term innovation culture
3M is a world-class product innovator. Best known for products like Post-it notes and Scotch tape, it has a history of innovation success in diverse fields: computer disks and tape, industrial coatings and abrasives, medical supplies, and office products. It began in 1901 as the Minnesota Mining and Manufacturing Corporation—and its first attempts at establishing the business were not successful. But the company persisted, and built a business that today sets a goal of getting 30 percent of its revenues from products introduced in the past three years. It has spent a 100 years refining its approach to innovation—and continues to succeed in doing so.

- Systematic and organized process: Innovation results from this process of managed change, turning new ideas into reality.

- Entrepreneurial skills: These lie at the heart of this process. But although "champions" who are passionate about change can make a lot happen, innovation is a team game, and managing it means involving people from across the organization.

- Creativity: This needs to be focused and directed.

- Understanding: Successful management of innovation needs a well-developed understanding of the process.

Factors in innovation success

- Planning: It depends on good project planning and management—against a background of uncertainty.

- Teamwork: It needs effective project team working—the ability to work with others under uncertain conditions.

- Leadership: Innovation requires strategic leadership—having a vision and being able to share it.

- Learning skills: Successful innovators have learning skills—the ability to analyze what works and why, and to use this knowledge to improve capability for the next time.

Innovation and invention

Innovation is often seen as simply coming up with a bright idea. The idea is certainly important, but by itself it is not sufficient. As an innovative manager you need to be able both to encourage new concepts and find ways to help make them happen.

TIP

ENCOURAGE SUGGESTIONS

Set up a suggestion box or an email address for employees to contribute their ideas.

Encouraging creative input

If innovation is about applied ideas, then you need to make sure that you have a plentiful supply of ideas to draw upon. Many organizations make the mistake of thinking that only certain people are capable of producing innovative ideas, and place the development of innovation in an area far away from the rest of the workforce. In fact, anyone involved in a process at any level is likely to have ideas about how it can be changed and improved. And since innovation is mostly about incremental ("doing what we do better") rather than radical change, even the most basic ideas can be worth considering. You should not attempt to limit innovation to research labs or in marketing meetings—it should be something to which everyone can contribute. Moreover, since innovation is a long process of making ideas work, you can make use of this creativity at every stage of the journey.

Developing an invention

Innovation is about ideas, but it is also about putting them into practice. While the inventor is a popular figure in marketing campaigns, in fact, many innovations come a long way from the initial idea before they become successful. Your creativity may be an essential starting point, but your task as a manager is to direct it to areas of your organization where it will be actively useful.

Balancing creativity and control

Another widespread myth is that innovation is solely about creativity—that all that is needed is an environment in which bright ideas can be explored. This is not true: it does not matter how many interesting ideas are flying around the place if nothing useful comes of them. Managing innovation is not only about unleashing creativity, but also about harnessing and focusing it. It is a balancing act—on the one hand releasing the flow of ideas to create and sharpen up innovations, and on the other making sure the ideas are focused toward actually delivering results that benefits the organization, without taking forever or consuming a vast budget. Managing innovation means balancing creativity with direction and control.

GET IDEAS REVIEWED

Make sure all suggestions are reviewed by more than one person, in case the initial reviewer misses any hidden potential.

HARNESSING CREATIVITY

FAST TRACK

OFF TRACK

FAST TRACK	OFF TRACK
Supporting creativity across the organization	Failing to implement good ideas
Investing in research and development	Creating new technologies without first ensuring they will be beneficial
Listening to customers to find out what innovations they want	Missing out on breakthrough innovations not yet conceived
Building a strong internal innovation infrastructure	Neglecting ideas from outside the organization
Using technology to solve product, process, and service problems	Focusing on technology and missing out on innovations

Making innovation happen

Once your innovative idea has been conceived and selected as worth pursuing, it needs to go through stages of development to make it a reality. It is important for any organization to have a standard process for developing innovations, particularly if you intend to make regular changes.

FIX THE STRUCTURE

Make sure your innovation structure is fixed before a project starts, and that all those involved are aware of the key stages.

Funneling innovation

The standard structure for the innovation process is to take your idea forward in stages. At each stage, the idea is reviewed to decide whether it is worth pursuing further. For every stage that it passes, an increasing amount of money, time, and resources must be dedicated to the project. This testing process is often described as a sort of a funnel. The mouth is wide, in that many ideas can begin the process, but more and more ideas will be rejected at each stage as they are shown to be unworkable for one reason or another. Only the very best ideas—those that are most likely to succeed—will ultimately make it into development.

The new-product development funnel

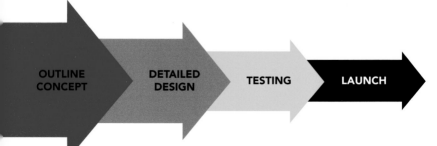

OUTLINE CONCEPT   DETAILED DESIGN   TESTING   LAUNCH

Mapping the route

There are four key stages that an idea must pass through before it enters the market or becomes a standard process. The first is the initial concept. A decision must be made as to whether the idea has the potential to benefit your organization, and whether the predicted costs merit further investment. The second stage is a detailed exploration of the practicalities—how the concept might work in practice, and, indeed, whether it is physically possible. At the same time, the concept must be developed so that you can discuss and share it with others, not least because along the way you'll have to convince some of them to provide funds, resources, and time to help you get it off the ground. The third phase is testing, which may include building a prototype, and researching how people in your target market (customers, clients, or coworkers) react to it. Finally, once testing is complete, the product can be launched, but even after launch its performance must be monitored to ensure your innovation provides the promised benefits.

Structuring the process

Managing an innovation through this process requires a well-defined structure, especially if you want to repeat the process and keep on generating and implementing new products, services, and processes. Not only must you establish each stage of the journey in detail, and provide a support structure to make sure your idea continues to progress, but you must also establish procedures for reviewing the project at each stage— and sometimes in between stages—to ensure that it remains on track and is still worth further investment. All of these procedures require resources, and your plan should include providing money, materials, and trained personnel to make innovation projects progress.

HOW TO...
PLAN THE PROCESS

Chart out a clear pathway along which innovation can proceed.

Fix key stages: initial idea, development, testing, launch.

Allocate resources: money, time, skills, and knowledge.

Appoint a leader and team to take your projects on the journey.

Fix points to assess projects before granting more resources.

Meeting challenges

Innovation is about adapting to an environment that is always turbulent and often hostile. It is not enough for a manager simply to cope with today's challenges—you need to be thinking about the challenges that will face your organization in the near future.

Expecting the unexpected

Like human beings, organizations tend to view the world in terms of what they expect. Contemporary business is extremely complicated, and seemingly distant changes can suddenly turn out to have a huge impact close to home, as the 2008–09 global financial crisis amply demonstrated. While, for the most part, your organization can rely upon established models, radical changes in the business environment do sometimes occur, and innovation is essential to coping with them. It is vital for the innovative manager to consider not only how to innovate when things are going well, but also when they are going badly. Some current factors that have the potential to upset established business models include:

• Climate change
• Sustainability of energy, and waste disposal
• Increase in digital commerce and telecommunications
• Social trends such as an aging population in western Europe and the US
• Shift in economic power to emerging markets
• The rise of consumerism in developing nations, especially those with large populations

Dealing with the unexpected

Dealing with the unexpected is part of the innovation challenge—in some ways the most important part, as unexpected challenges can prove life-threatening to an organization. From Henry Ford working on "a car for Everyman," to the IT specialists who moved banking, insurance, and stock trading online from paper, or the revolution in the music and entertainment industry caused by Internet file sharing, new business models are constantly emerging. And in each case, established players were severely damaged because they responded too slowly, leaving the door open for new competitors, some of whom have become today's major players. To combat this, innovation managers should always try to answer the following questions:
• How can you search at the edge of your organization's radar for problems and opportunities?
• How can you make sure your message gets listened to and acted upon when something important occurs?
• How can you implement innovations that are totally different from anything you have done in the past?

TIP

RESEARCH CHALLENGES

Be aware of areas in which proposed innovations could help make your organization both more vulnerable and more resistant to outside challenges.

✔ CHECKLIST **PREPARING FOR CHALLENGES**

	YES	NO
• Does the organization's management create "stretch goals" that provide the direction but not the route for innovation?	☐	☐
• Do you actively explore the future, making use of tools and techniques like scenarios and foresight?	☐	☐
• Do you have the capacity to challenge your current position— do you think about how your business could be adversely affected?	☐	☐
• Do you have strategic decision-making and project selection mechanisms to deal with radical proposals?	☐	☐
• Do you have, and make, connections across your industry to provide your organization with fresh perspectives?	☐	☐
• Do you have alerting mechanisms to warn you about new trends?	☐	☐

Chapter 2

Planning for innovation

Every organization needs to innovate to keep pace with a changing world. But unless you know where, what, and why you want to change, your blueprint for innovation will come to nothing. Careful planning is essential for successful innovation.

Innovating strategically

Developing a roadmap for change, or an innovation strategy, can help your organization stay ahead of the competition over the long term. Any innovation project involves resources—money, time, employees' skills—and you need to spend these wisely if an innovation is to be worthwhile.

BACK UP YOUR DECISIONS

Make sure all your decisions have sound strategic backing in line with the wide aims of the organization.

Developing a strategy

An innovation strategy requires three key elements:
- **Strategic analysis:** what *could* you do, and why would that make a difference?
- **Strategic decision-making:** what *are* you going to do, and why are you choosing that option over others?
- **Strategic action:** how can you make sure the project happens, and support and review it as the innovation takes shape? Some of the most important innovation decisions are not about starting projects, but scrapping those which looked good at the outset but which then failed to develop as expected.

Innovating internally

An overall innovation strategy matters if you are competing with other organizations in the marketplace. But it is just as important to have a strategy inside the organization, to help prioritize changes you make to the ways you do things—or process innovation. This will help you to avoid a situation where you spend your energy improving irrelevant details while leaving the really important changes undone—a bit like rearranging the deckchairs on the *Titanic*.

Innovating across the board

It is not just commercial organizations that need an innovation strategy. Our public services desperately need creative ideas for change to deal with problems like education, healthcare, transportation—but simply spending scarce taxpayers' money on any project that looks interesting is not a good recipe for long-term improvement in those services. We need focused change, targeted at what will make a real difference. And they need the discipline to manage what can be huge projects: to complete them on time and within budget, and, if necessary, to kill them off before they become potential high-profile disasters.

TIP

BUILD A VISION

Make sure people understand the "big picture"— what you are trying to achieve with innovation. Once it's clear what the challenge is, they can contribute their creativity and energy to help make it happen.

CASE STUDY

Innovation with impact

India's Aravind Eye Clinics revolutionized treatment of eye problems like cataracts, which caused preventable blindness for around 45 million people. The operation to treat it is relatively simple but costs around $300—well out of the reach of the rural poor. But through a systematic series of process innovations targeted at reducing cost without compromising quality, the average cost came down to $25. This sustained pattern of innovation continues, and with around 250,000 operations performed every year, these clinics have become "best practice" centers for such surgery, with doctors coming from around the world to learn from them.

Modelling innovation

To plan for innovation, you need some way to map the different possible directions, in order to apply resources and energy appropriately. One useful model for this is the innovation compass, which plots innovation along two axes: doing things better, and doing things differently.

Using the innovation compass

As we have seen, innovation can be radical or incremental, and can proceed in one of four directions: product or service, process, market, or business model. The innovation compass maps all these variables against each other, allowing you to work out where innovation efforts in your organization are concentrated, and where they are neglected. Each of the four points of the compass represents one of the innovation directions. Incremental innovations sit closer to the center, while radical innovations are placed farther away. Plotting all of your innovation projects on a graph helps you direct innovation to the areas of your organization where it will be most useful.

Defining your innovation

The compass defines the "innovation space" your organization needs to explore to help move it forward. A number of journeys can be taken, not just along the four main directions, but in combination. For example, you could introduce a new product that opens up a new market, as Nintendo did with the Wii and the DS, targeting people who had never played computer games before. Or you could apply a radical procedure as McDonald's did, opening up the fast food market by applying lessons from Henry Ford's mass production process innovation in car making.

RADICAL BUSINESS MODEL INNOVATION
Apple's iTunes and iPod systems, which changed the music industry.

RADICAL PRODUCT INNOVATION
White LED (light-emitting diode) lighting that led to a shift in energy efficiency.

INCREMENTAL BUSINESS MODEL INNOVATION
Rolls Royce's after-sales support that emphasized service and support.

INCREMENTAL PRODUCT INNOVATION
The first flat beds on transatlantic business class airline routes.

Types of innovation

INCREMENTAL PROCESS INNOVATION
NHS Direct in the UK, which began offering health advice over the telephone.

INCREMENTAL MARKET INNOVATION
Low-cost single-use shampoo packets for low-income Indian households.

RADICAL PROCESS INNOVATION
Online banking and insurance made the delivery of financial services automatic and cheaper.

RADICAL MARKET INNOVATION
Low-cost airlines that made flying available to a whole new market of flyers.

Applying strategic analysis

The innovation compass can help you look at possible directions, but you also need to plan in ways that help you move ahead of your competitors. You can do this through a strategic analysis of your market situation, to see if your proposed innovations have the potential to give you an advantage.

Profiling your innovation

One way to do this involves profiling the planned innovations against what the market wants and what your best competitors can offer. Building such profiles step by step can provide a focus for shared discussion and bring in different perspectives from across the organization. Strategy is rarely about "right" answers—there's too much uncertainty about innovation to make that possible. So you need to explore as widely as possible to get a "good" answer. Doing this well means collecting different views and information. More minds on the job improves your overall knowledge and helps build support for your decisions.

Winning market share

*Order qualifiers
—*factors that attract people to your product or service in the marketplace.*

*Order winners
—*factors that determine whether people will buy your product or service.*

In any marketplace, some basic requirements—"order qualifiers"*—must be met just to stay in the game. If your prices are twice those of your direct competitor, you are unlikely to do much business. But when everyone offers the same price, what will differentiate your product is the something extra you offer—higher quality, more features, sleeker design. Order qualifiers are your entry into the marketplace, but order winners* are what determine whether people buy from you or not. You need to have an idea of both: whether your planned innovation is simply catching up (basic order qualifier) or moving ahead (creating an order winner).

Plotting an innovation profile

Having identified the order qualifiers and order winners in your target market, use market research to plot them on a simple graph against their importance to consumers. Then develop a scoring system for how well you and your competitors meet these requirements, and add the lines. This will give you a simple outline of where your strengths and opportunities lie in a given market. In the example, you are behind your competitor, so you either close the gap, or exit from the market.

KEEP UP-TO-DATE

Make sure you base your analysis on the most recent market research.

Measuring your performance

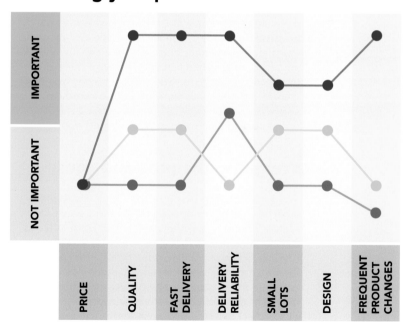

- ● **What the market wants**
- ● **How well you actually perform**
- ● **How well your best competitor performs**

Choosing the right options

Using these ideas helps you see what your options are, and how they would help your organization. But you still need to decide which of these options to choose, and justify that decision. Each option you pursue views opportunity costs in time and money, so it is important to select only the most promising ideas to pursue.

DECIDE OBJECTIVELY
Use some form of check on innovation projects before you start on them. Will the reward you expect be worth the risk and cost of the project?

Deciding where to innovate

So how do you decide on this? You could just run with the ideas that attract you and act on your hunches. That is a little like a gambler throwing the chips down randomly or backing a horse in a race because they have a "feeling" about it. Or you could use a more systematic approach. You can never make innovation a cast-iron certainty, because there is too much uncertainty involved—will the technology work, is there a market, will the competition introduce something else before us? But you can convert the uncertainty into some form of calculated risk.

Weighing the pros and cons

The easiest way to do this is through a cost-benefit analysis—simply comparing how much benefit the idea will bring against how much it will cost in terms of resources. That might give you an overall feel for one project over another, but a more useful approach is some form of "decision matrix" that helps you compare many different alternatives on a number of cost and benefit dimensions. Sometimes, looking at a project in just narrow cash terms may mean you miss out on some of its other potential benefits, like entering a new market, or learning some new skills, that you could then use in future projects.

Formulating a decision matrix

The decision matrix allows you to give objective scores to each innovation option, to help you make better decisions about which will be most beneficial for your business. The matrix itself can be drawn as a simple table. List the options that are competing for strategic support (A, B, C) along the X-axis, then list the key checks along the Y-axis. Key checks can include such factors as: Does the idea fit with what you already know (your competence base)? Does it fit your overall business strategy? And how feasible do you think it would be to implement it?

Decision matrix—
a tool to help
you make innovation
decisions by
balancing risk and
reward dimensions
across several
different criteria.

You can fill these cells in with simple scores or with detailed comments. Add columns to rate the expected costs and benefits associated with the different projects, then add a total score column that tries to arrive at some priority based on the individual cells. You can continue adding cells, depending on the range of criteria you want to satisfy. Most decision matrices use a "rough cut" version to knock out options with low potential, and then repeat the exercise with more columns to narrow the selection.

✔ CHECKLIST MAKING A DECISION MATRIX

	YES	NO
• Have you established a definitive list of the options competing for strategic support?	☐	☐
• Do you have a list of key checks that must be applied to each option, and do the key checks cover all aspects of the innovation's potential benefits?	☐	☐
• Have you considered all potential costs that you might incur as you pursue this innovation?	☐	☐
• Are some factors more important than others, and, if so, have you weighted their scores appropriately (say, by doubling the points)?	☐	☐
• What other disruptive factors could your ideas face in the future?	☐	☐

Building a strategic portfolio

All but the smallest organizations are likely to want to include more than one innovation project in their strategy. While a decision matrix helps you compare projects, you also need diversity in your innovation portfolio. Portfolio management helps you to achieve this.

TIP

HEDGE YOUR BETS

Aim to reach a balance across your portfolio between risks and rewards, so that you have a mixture of probable successes and more risky—but potentially more profitable—experiments.

Balancing your portfolio

For a balanced portfolio you need a mix of decision criteria: the risk of failure must be balanced with the rewards of success. This requires analysis of potential obstacles against potential benefits. In general, a safe innovation will be based on what your company does well. More risky innovations are radical in nature. While the risks of such innovations are greater, the potential rewards are also significantly more attractive. You may decide to back a couple of high-risk projects if they are small because they could move you to a new game— and if they fail only a small amount of resources will be wasted—but it would be foolish to base all your hopes of progress on risky ventures that may never work out.

Gaining an overview

TIP

It is useful to develop an overview of your portfolio not just in terms of the risks and rewards, but also in terms of how much you are allocating to each project. This can be done by using a bubble chart, which is generated by plotting your projects as circles on a graph against potential risk and potential reward. The more resources a project requires, the larger its corresponding circle on the chart. This chart gives you an instant view of what resources are allocated to what levels of risk and reward. It can show you immediately if you have too many resources tied up in risky projects that are unlikely to succeed in the end. Equally, you can see if you are putting too much investment in a safe bet that is unlikely to generate significant rewards.

BE FAIR

Scrutinize all innovation projects equally and fairly. Do not start up a project just because one individual wants it to happen.

MANAGING YOUR PORTFOLIO

FAST TRACK

OFF TRACK

FAST TRACK	OFF TRACK
The number of innovation projects in progress at any one time is limited	There is no limit to the projects you can take on, so you spread your resources too thinly
Innovation projects have targets and are abandoned if targets are not met	You are reluctant to kill off projects if they are not working out
Priority is given to innovations that meet strategic goals	Unimportant projects succeed at the cost of strategically valuable innovations
Innovation projects are subject to careful selection	You do not have a clear criteria for selecting projects

Promoting ideas for change

Unless you are a top manager in your organization, chances are that you will need to "sell" your ideas for change at some point. Maybe you are an entrepreneur pitching an idea to a potential investor, or you have a great idea about how to make things work more efficiently in your organization. In either case, you will need support if your idea is to become a reality.

Making the business case

Whatever the starting point, the destination will be the same: you need to convince someone else that your idea is great and that it will work, and that they will get their investment (of time and money) back. And they need to believe in you and your capacity to deliver all of this. The problem is that you believing in your idea is unlikely to be enough—you need to put together a compelling business case to convince others that your idea has practical potential.

TIP

REHEARSE YOUR PITCH

Practice "selling" your idea to others, inviting critical comments and suggestions for how to improve it. Anticipating the big questions before you make the pitch to decision-makers will help ensure your message gets across.

Gaining support

Organizations need to innovate, but they cannot do everything. They need to explore options and then make tough decisions about which ideas they will back and why. You can influence these decisions to your advantage—if you know your organization is trying to put together a portfolio of projects that balances risk and reward, you can try and make them include yours in the mix. But you need to present your idea in such a way that its merits are clear. Ask yourself how you can engage them—can you show them a prototype so they can add their comments? Do you have the answers to questions they might ask you? And do you come across as being passionate about the project—will they believe in you?

Covering all the angles

Making a compelling business case is at the heart of innovation. Decisions will not get made on the basis of personality and passion alone—you need to be able to convince decision-makers to spend resources on a project that will work. Is there a market, will the technology work, can you protect the idea, what will it cost, and what are the likely benefits? Showing that you have thought the project through and have answers to any difficult questions they might throw at you will enhance your chances of a successful pitch.

BUILDING A GOOD BUSINESS CASE

FEATURE	WHAT TO INCLUDE
Outline your idea	A short and simple explanation of your idea—how it is new and what it will do. Remember it is not what you think but how "they" see it, so try and present it in terms of what it will do for them. You might try mapping it on a strategic position map.
Market analysis	Who is it targeted at? Who wants it, why do they need it, and why don't they have it yet? How big is this market? Is it growing, declining, or static?
Competitors	Who else is out there, what do they offer, how will this idea get ahead of them, how might they react, and how do you protect yourself from that?
Why it will work	What do you know, and what prior knowledge, skills, experience, and networks can you bring to the table?
Rewards	What will you get if you succeed—money, market share, customer satisfaction—and how long you will have to wait until you get them?
Costs	How much will it cost, and what do you need to make it happen?
Risk factors	What might pose problems and how will you get around them?
Project management	Who will take this forward and how? What reassurances can you offer that you can do it?

Making real-time decisions

1
INITIAL TRIGGER
An idea for a new product appears. Should it be explored further?

Innovation is about uncertainty, and so the ability to review and change your decisions over time is crucial. To make a decision and then commit all of your resources to it without having the option of changing plans midway is risky. The longer a project goes on, the more resources are put at risk if it fails.

Allocating resources

2
CONCEPT DEFINITION
Information sought on technology, markets. Does it make business sense?

Smart organizations know that turning an idea into reality is a learning process. As you move through the project you discover new things about the technology, about the market you thought existed, about your competitors. So it makes sense to view the journey in stages, and to increase resources allocated at each stage, from outline concept through to the eventual launch of the product.

Using stage-gate reviews

3
FEASIBILITY STUDIES
Market surveys are conducted. Should it enter full-scale development?

A widely used approach, originally developed by Robert Cooper, a Canadian professor, is to introduce strategic decision points at various stages in the process. Instead of making a one-time decision at the start, this "stage-gate" approach sets up a series of decision points, each tougher than the last. Key questions are asked at each stage, and only if the answers are met does the gate open so that resources flow to support the next stage of development.

A sample
stage-gate
model

5

DECIDING TO LAUNCH
Final go-ahead for
mainstream manufacturing
and marketing.

4

DESIGN DEVELOPMENT
Prototype developed.
Should it enter
full-scale production?

Chapter 3

Making innovation happen

Innovation is more than a great idea—innovation succeeds only when you put that idea into action. The innovative manager needs the ability to find and select good ideas, put them into operation, and persuade users to adopt them.

Moving toward innovation

You can look at innovation as a journey: from the spark of a new idea to seeing that idea realized in the form of a new product, service, or workflow. You could get lucky with it once, but if you are going to repeat it, you need to put in place a systematic process to make it happen consistently.

TIP

BUILD A ROADMAP FOR THE JOURNEY

Mapping out how you will take the idea ahead helps identify potential problems and who or what else you will need to help deal with them.

Finding and selecting ideas

The journey starts with a trigger signal—a bright idea, a customer need, catching up with a competitor. Whatever the stimulus, the challenge in managing your innovation process at this stage is to make sure you have in place ways of searching for and picking up the signals. But you can't do everything—you need to be able to answer the question: "Of all the things we could do, what are we going to do, and why?" You need to select—to make choices based on where you are trying to get to as an organization and how the proposed innovation might help you get there.

Implementing ideas

Next, you have the challenge of implementing the innovation possibility—to make the new product or service come alive, to bring the new way of doing things into shape. This is all about project management, but against a background of uncertainty. You won't know whether you can actually make the technology work, or if there will be a market for your new product or service, until you try to make it happen. So you need a structure that allows you to monitor progress, and, if necessary, stop projects before they go too far ahead.

Reviewing the system

When you have gotten as far as a working model or a prototype of the new service or process, you need to make sure people will actually adopt it. Not every new idea finds a home, and the challenge at this stage in the process is making sure you can get sufficient uptake to make a difference. If you are really going to make this an innovation system—one that delivers a steady stream of new products, processes, and services—you need to make sure you learn from your mistakes and modify the system so you can do it better the next time.

 IN FOCUS... LEARNING FROM MISTAKES

Sometimes great ideas come from mistakes and apparent failures. 3M's Post-it notes began when a polymer chemist mixed an experimental batch of adhesive that turned out to be quite weak. This failure in terms of the original project provided the impetus for what is now a billion dollar product platform for the company. In the late 1980s, scientists working for Pfizer began testing compound UK-92480 for the treatment of angina. Although it showed little benefit in clinical trials on humans, the team pursued an interesting side effect that led to UK-92480 becoming the drug Viagra.

Looking for ideas

The first stage in practical innovation is gathering ideas for new projects. Innovation can be triggered by many different pressures, and to manage it effectively you must have mechanisms to pick up on these pressures. These can come from within your organization, or from the wider world.

HOW TO... SEARCH FOR IDEAS

Explore existing technology to find opportunity.

↓

Research the potential market for your product.

↓

Investigate your competition and learn from them.

↓

Look at threats and opportunities for your business.

↓

Use stakeholders' ideas for new perspectives.

Pushing the frontiers

New developments in science have always pushed the frontiers of knowledge and created opportunities for innovation. Use the Internet or "knowledge brokers" to help cast the search net widely. With nearly $1 trillion being spent every year on R&D around the world, the problem is less one of knowledge creation than one of tapping into existing research. Conduct your own technological research—creating new knowledge—or tap into research being done elsewhere, such as at universities or research institutes. Working with other organizations will help you share the costs and risks.

Meeting demand

Necessity is the mother of invention, so making sure you understand user needs will help you pick up clear signals for innovation. Getting close to actual or potential customers and understanding their needs will help you understand user needs. Market research is one good source of this, as are customer service and complaint records. Needs are not just about external markets for products and services—demand pull works inside the organization as well, as a driver of process innovation. Pay attention to sources of frustration highlighted by your workforce, and plan innovation to ease them.

Getting ideas from users

A potential source of innovation can be frustration: the frustration experienced by users who want something additional or different from the products and services they use. This can be channeled to create ideas and prototypes for innovations.

For example, Linux is not a product developed by a large corporation, but the result of collaboration among a community of users who wanted software that better suited their needs, and they continue improving and updating it. Going to an older example: the pickup truck was not invented in Detroit by the large American car companies, but emerged on farms where farmers had bought the early trucks, stripped out the seats, taken off the roof, and improvised a truck more suited to their farm needs. Work with "lead users" to capture their insights and prototypes. During process innovation inside the organization, use suggestion programs to capture employee ideas. Use web communities—or "crowd sourcing"—to help create ideas for innovation or improve on what is already there.

TIP

REVIEW RELEVANCE

As your project progresses, keep monitoring not only expenditure and performance, but also its continuing relevance to end users. Otherwise you may find yourself with a perfectly executed innovation that your customers no longer want.

CASE STUDY

Getting ideas from outside

Procter and Gamble (P&G) used to spend around $3 billion each year on technology research, and employed more than 7,000 people to carry it out. However, it has now committed to sourcing half of its innovations from outside the company. In doing so, it has had to develop completely new ways of working, sharing its unused ideas with a wider world, and picking up on other people's ideas in the most unlikely of places. For example, the idea of Pringles potato chips having messages printed on them was made a reality not by P&G research scientists but by connecting with a small bakery in Bologna, Italy, that had developed a special edible ink and a spraying process for the ink. The connection was made through one of the increasing number of Internet knowledge broker sites—a kind of eBay for innovation.

Tapping the future

TIP

**CONSIDER
ALL FACTORS**
Take account of
current events in your
future planning even
if they do not seem
to affect you directly.
Remember that
innovations can
come from any area.

Looking at a selection of alternatives often provides clues about new innovation possibilities. Tools you can use to do this include trend extrapolation—where you research market or performance trends and make future plans on the assumption that those trends will continue—and forecasting tools such as economic planning. You could gather panels of experts (also known as "Delphi panels") to discuss the most likely outcomes of current events and help you tailor your plans to expected developments. You can even write your own "science-fiction" stories about alternative futures to explore the possibilities, and how your organization might respond to them.

Benchmarking for improvement

Looking at what other companies do and comparing them to your own organization can give insights into new directions for product, process, or service innovations. This approach is known as "benchmarking." It aids you in comparative profiling of products and services. Benchmarking processes can be undertaken between similar activities within the same organization, between similar activities in different divisions of a large organization, between similar activities in different firms within a sector, and between similar activities in different firms and sectors. Compare your products and processes with those of other firms systematically and regularly.

Finding inspiration from outside

In addition to benchmarking by observing other companies, you may choose to collaborate with them directly to develop new ideas. As a manager, you should develop external networks of people who can help provide ideas—those with specialized knowledge, for example. You can also work closely with lead users—clients, customers, or employees at the forefront of innovation—to develop new products and services. A final source of ideas are your own mistakes, and those of your competitors. When a project flops, or a team underperforms, examine how this came about and consider what innovations could protect you against similar failures.

ASK YOURSELF... HOW OPEN TO INNOVATION IS YOUR ORGANIZATION?

- Do you have good relationships with your suppliers and pick up a steady stream of ideas from them?
- Are you good at understanding the needs of your customers/end users?
- Do you work well with universities and other research centers to help you develop your knowledge?
- Are your people involved in suggesting ideas for improvements to products or processes?
- Do you look ahead in a structured way (using forecasting tools and techniques) to try and imagine future threats and opportunities?

Making a strategic selection

Effective innovators choose projects on the basis of clear ground rules. Use techniques and structures to help you in the selection process, and make sure these are flexible enough to help monitor and adapt projects over time as ideas become concrete innovations. If a project doesn't perform, you should have mechanisms in place either to rethink it or scrap it altogether.

TIP

SET CLEAR DECISION CRITERIA

There are plenty of opportunities for innovation, so make sure you have some clear decision criteria to help choose the best options.

Analyzing the options

Strategic analysis is about gaining strategic advantage through innovation. It means making sure you know where you are in terms of overall strategy. And it means knowing what you can realistically make happen—what knowledge, experience, and resources can you bring to bear? If you are an ice-cream salesman, then moving into nuclear power to capitalize on growing energy demand may be a nice idea, but not feasible. But moving into a new range of food products that could be delivered door-to-door would build on your experience and knowledge and be a good bet.

Choosing projects

When considering a potential innovation project, there are three important questions to ask: First, does the idea have promise—does it have achievable potential to improve your organization? Second, is it a good fit with your wider business strategy? There is no sense pursuing an innovation to improve a product strand that is being phased out, for example. An idea should also be considered looking at risk and reward in your overall innovation portfolio. Finally, does the idea build on skills and resources that your organization possesses and can take advantage of? And, if not, can you obtain the knowledge and expertise required to make it work?

Implementing your choice

TIP

The process of implementing an innovation is about project management—making something happen within a budget and to a set timescale. Strategic implementation means thinking about the downstream side of this—can you actually make it happen? Do you have the knowledge and skills that you need—or if not, do you know where to get them? Remember that many innovations involve making strategic alliances, so not having knowledge and skills in-house is not necessarily a barrier here. Have you thought about change-management issues—how to ensure that people elsewhere in the organization will buy in to your planned change? And how will you organize your team to make the innovation happen—who will lead, what balance of skills and experience do you require, and how will you build a high-performing team to deliver the project? All these factors must be considered in advance to give your innovation the best chance of success.

MANAGE RISK
Make sure you monitor and review your projects regularly as they develop over time. Set clear criteria for success at that stage, and if projects are not working out, do not be afraid to close them down.

✔ CHECKLIST HANDLING INNOVATIVE IDEAS

	YES	NO
• Do you have a clear system for choosing innovation projects?	☐	☐
• Does someone who has a good idea know how to take it forward?	☐	☐
• Do you balance your portfolio with low- and high-risk projects?	☐	☐
• Do you focus on a mixture of innovation with regard to product, process, market, and business model?	☐	☐
• Can you balance "do better" and "do different" innovation?	☐	☐
• Do you recognize the need to work outside of the box?	☐	☐
• Do you have a system to handle off-center but interesting ideas?	☐	☐
• Do you have a structure for corporate venturing?	☐	☐

Developing your idea

Having picked your idea and decided to back it as an innovation project, you now have the challenge of turning it into a real product, service, or process for people. This is where you need to put in place structures and systems to help manage projects effectively. But it's not just managing in terms of resources and budgets—there is also the challenge of uncertainty.

TIP

BE FLEXIBLE
Allow sufficient flexibility in the system for small, fast-track projects to take place.

Managing the process

In innovation there is no such thing as guaranteed success—you might find out after you start that the technology that looked so exciting at the start actually doesn't work or do what you want it to do. Or else you might find that the market you thought was there for your new idea actually isn't that interested. Or maybe a competitor has come up on your blind side and offered something better. Or the government has changed the rules of the game on you. Or some other unexpected thing has happened—remember Murphy's Law—if something can go wrong it probably will.

All of this means that you need to have good project-management practices as your innovation develops, and also the flexibility to review and change your projects—to cancel those that are going nowhere, to modify others to meet changes in circumstances, and to continue to support only those that look like they are really going to produce real benefits. You need a project management system that regularly reviews the status of projects, identifies the risks associated with progressing them further, and only allocates additional resources to those projects that still meet strategic criteria and have a high probability of success.

Choosing the right method

Innovations come in all shapes and sizes. You need to think about different project types—is it a simple incremental development or a radical breakthrough? Does it need people from different areas to cooperate and share knowledge or can it be done by a small group from the same department? Is it a joint venture with other organizations? Is it something completely different from anything you have done before and needs different ways of working? You can think about a number of options on a spectrum of project structures to help deal with each of these:

• **In-line structures:** carried out within the established group or by an individual as part of their work.
• **Matrix structures:** where people work some time on the project and the rest on their mainstream job.
• **Dedicated project team:** people work full time on the project and have dedicated resources.
• **Breakthrough or "skunk works" team:** the team operates independently of the main organization.

CASE STUDY

Making it relevant

The Ford Edsel was one of Ford's best-researched product concepts ever. Market analysis had led Ford to believe that a new luxury car priced in between its two nearest rivals would be an instant hit. The car was developed at great expense, hyped with aggressive marketing, and released with much fanfare in 1957, but the final product failed. The Edsel was conceived during the economic growth of the early 1950s. By the time of its release in 1957, the US was on the brink of a recession, and consumers were turning to smaller, cheaper cars. The demands of the market altered. The Edsel remains a classic example of the dangers of not reviewing an innovation process.

TIP

Applying necessary expertise

SHARE RESULTS
Ensure that the results of procedures such as prototype testing and market research are shared across all teams involved in a project, so that everyone is aware of potential problems.

Taking ideas through from conception to successful implementation involves bringing together multiple knowledge sets through a series of phases staged over time. It is important to ensure that all necessary skill sets are involved in the process along the way. One way of doing this is to run it as a simple sequential process, with responsibility for the project moving to different functional groups in the organization as it progresses. For example, in developing a physical product, the sequence might be:

• Marketing team initiates a new product concept.
• R&D team studies feasibility and demand.
• Small-scale production team develops and tests a prototype.
• Production department begins full-scale manufacture.
• Sales and marketing begin to promote the product that is ready for launch.

This model works a little like a relay race, with one group passing the baton on to the next, and may be suitable for projects where time is not a factor, and the success of the project is uncertain in the initial stages.

ASK YOURSELF... HOW WELL DOES YOUR ORGANIZATION MANAGE IMPLEMENTATION?

• Do we have clear and well-understood formal processes in place, to help us manage new product development effectively from idea to launch?
• Are our innovation projects usually completed on time and within budget?
• Do we have effective mechanisms for managing process change, from idea through to successful implementation?
• Do we have mechanisms in place to ensure early involvement of all departments in developing new products and processes?
• Is there sufficient flexibility in our system for product development to allow small "fast track" projects to happen?
• Do our innovation teams involve people from all relevant divisions?

Managing implementation

A sequential process, however, risks missing out on key knowledge inputs from different groups, and it fails to take account of uncertainties that might emerge as you go through the project. It is also a slow process, since things cannot move to the next stage until they have completed the previous one. In practice, many activities can be done in parallel and with interaction between different functional groups working concurrently.

MAKING A SUCCESS OF IMPLEMENTATION

KEY AIDS	HOW THEY HELP
Systematic process for progressing new products	• Provides stage-wise monitoring and evaluation.
Early involvement of all relevant functions	• Brings key perspectives into the process early enough to influence design and prepare for problems later in the process. • Increases efficiency by detecting problems early.
Overlapping/parallel working	• Concurrent or simultaneous engineering aids faster development while retaining cross-functional involvement.
Appropriate project management structures	• Allows choice of structure—matrix/line/project/heavyweight project management—to suit conditions and task.
Cross-functional team working	• Involves different perspectives. • Ensures effective team-working and develops capabilities in flexible problem-solving.
Advanced support tools	• Use of tools—such as computer-aided design, rapid prototyping, and computer-supported cooperative work aids—assists with quality and speed of development.
Learning and continuous improvement	• Encourages carrying forward lessons learned—through things like post-project audits. • Develops a continuous improvement culture.

Diffusing your innovation

A great idea implemented perfectly will be of no use to your organization if no one adopts it. A new product must be bought by customers if it is to succeed in the marketplace, and a new procedure must be followed by employees for it to have any effect. To manage your innovation journey to the end, be sure you've done enough to make people adopt your new idea.

TIP

IDENTIFY EARLY ADOPTERS

Keep an eye out for people willing to engage with new products or processes and invite them to participate in testing.

Understanding adoption

No innovation is adopted all at once. The process is cumulative: initially only a few people take a new idea on board. They are gradually joined by more and more users until the last few percent trickle in at the end of the process. A graph of percentage adopters against time takes on a characteristic S-shaped curve.

A key message from this is to work with potential early adopters at as soon a stage as possible. Getting them involved in testing and trials, learning from their feedback, and building their ideas into the final innovation can help kick the adoption curve upward. This is where tools like prototyping are useful, giving potential adopters the chance to see, touch, and play with an idea before it is finalized, so you can get their reactions and ideas to help improve it.

early bird

market

feedback

beta

prototype

trial version

Getting people involved

"Test marketing" of a new product or service helps explore customer preferences that provide information about things like pricing policy or advertising, and checks if people really want the new offering. Such testing also offers the chance to test different launch strategies—for example, two different regions could be used, each employing a different launch strategy.

The same principle holds for process innovations inside the organization—changes in "the way we do things around here." Getting the ideas and insights of people who will be using the new process is an ideal way of improving the final design of the process as well as smoothing the route to change.

TIP

MAKE USE OF TESTERS

When implementing a new procedure, invite those involved in the testing to help train and support new users.

Maximizing your chances

Three factors determine the speed at which an innovation diffuses: the nature of the innovation (radical innovations are adopted more slowly than small ones), the characteristics of the adopter (some communities are more receptive to change), and the personality of the innovator. It makes sense to allow more time and resources to promote a radical change in a conservative community than a small change in a flexible workforce.

share   preferences   try   adopt   potential   test   product

**HOW TO...
MAKE A
NEW IDEA
POPULAR**

Widely publicize
the benefits
before launch.

Offer sneak
previews, trials, or
training sessions.

Get early users
to persuade
other people.

Use your user
feedback to
adapt innovation.

Listing characteristics

Certain key characteristics greatly affect how easily
an innovation can be diffused. The first is relative
advantage: how much better the new innovation
is perceived to be. People will be more eager to
adopt an idea if its benefits are obvious. Balanced
against this is complexity: the more difficult people
perceive the innovation to be (the more complex the
procedure, the more technical the product) the less
likely they will be to adopt it. Other important factors
are visibility—it can be useful to offer demonstrations
of the benefits of your new idea—and whether it
can be trialed—training and trial runs are important
to help users come to terms with new products and
procedures. Finally, the product must be compatible
with the market—it must fit the people who you
want to adopt it. Try to minimize any mismatch by
developing variants for different groups of user.

Understanding early adopters

Innovation adoption is a complex negotiation
between proponents of an innovation and the people
they want to use it. Some people can be relied upon
to be enthusiastic and try out new products, while
others will resist changes to their settled preferences.
To accelerate diffusion of your innovation you need to
know the types of adopter and what motivates them.
Your best friends will be innovators—cutting-edge
users who are always willing to try new products and
processes. They can be recruited during testing stages,
working with prototypes and beta versions, and may
also come up with ideas for improvement. The next
are early adopters—trendsetters in a community whom
others imitate. They are often open to good new ideas,
and should be targeted because if you can appeal to
them and meet their needs, others are likely to follow.

Understanding slower adopters

The early majority is the large group of people ready to adopt an innovation when it appears to be taking off, and when they witness the advantages enjoyed by early adopters. Positive experiences by early adopters can encourage the early majority to come on board. The late majority consists of the more conservative members of the group who are only prepared to change when they can see a large population already successfully using the innovation. You can best reach them by promoting positive experiences reported by earlier adopters. Finally, any community will include laggards—a few people extremely resistant to change. A lot of effort will be required to convince these people, and you may decide to leave them be if 100 percent adoption is not essential to your innovation.

SELLING YOUR IDEA

FAST TRACK	**OFF TRACK**
Communicating in terms that your prospective users recognize	Use jargon and specialized language
Understanding their world—seeing the innovation through their eyes	Making assumptions that they can see the benefits the way you do
Listening to their concerns—and if possible build their ideas, wishes, and needs into the final version	Presenting them with a "take it or leave it" solution and ignoring their feedback
Developing a relationship with them: engage them as partners in the development of the innovation	Treating them as passive end-users and expecting them simply to do as they are told

Chapter 4

Building the innovative organization

Innovation is about human creativity and ingenuity—piecing together a puzzle, solving problems, and creating solutions. Developing and implementing new ideas can work only when backed by an innovative organization—one geared to change.

Laying the foundations

The innovation system provides the structure for an idea, and strategy directs it, but it is people who actually make it progress. However, just throwing people at the innovation challenge is not enough: you need to provide a context in which they use their creativity and share their ideas.

Avoiding chaos

*Skunk works— *a group within an organization whose role is to work on advanced projects and develop prototypes with minimal restrictions.*

Blueprints for an innovative organization will highlight the need to eliminate stifling bureaucracy, unhelpful structures, communication barriers, and other factors that stop ideas from getting through. But you must be careful not to fall into the chaos trap—not all innovation works in loose, informal, and organic environments, or "skunk works"*, and these types of organizations can often end up obstructing successful innovation. Successful entrepreneurs and innovative organizations know this, and use a range of structures, tools, and techniques to balance formal and organic structures.

Balancing the structure

There are a number of considerations that can help you to strike this balance. First, while an appropriate structure is essential for an innovation idea to progress, rigid hierarchies can stifle new ideas, as employees at lower levels find themselves unable to pass their suggestions on to management. Cooperation across team boundaries is essential, since input from many different skill sets will be needed to implement a new idea—this cannot be achieved if each department operates on its own. Good communication across the organization is equally important, as well as communication up and down the hierarchy, so that ideas can be shared, and no one feels left out as an innovation moves forward. The structure of individual teams is also important. Effective team-working means that ideas are discussed and developed within a team, and all team members are encouraged to contribute. Ensure that all teams are aware their input is welcome, rather than treating innovation as a job for the experts.

TIP

TRAIN YOUR EMPLOYEES

Make sure your staff receives necessary training to understand the innovation processes in which they are involved, since this will help them generate ideas and take on new processes easily.

ASK YOURSELF... DOES YOUR ORGANIZATION PROMOTE INNOVATION?

- Does the organizational structure facilitate innovation rather than stifling it?
- Do people work well together across departmental boundaries?
- Is there a strong commitment to training and development of people?
- Are our people involved in suggesting ideas for improvements to products or processes?
- Does our structure help us to make decisions rapidly?
- Is communication effective, and does it work top-down, bottom-up, and across the organization?
- Does our reward and recognition system support innovation?
- Do we have a supportive climate for new ideas, so that people do not have to leave the organization to make them happen?
- Do we work well in teams?

Setting an innovation culture

Any organization has its own particular patterns of behavior that are underpinned by values and beliefs—its organizational culture. If you want to develop an innovative organization, creating the right culture is the biggest challenge.

TIP

REWARD INNOVATIVE THINKING

Develop a recognition-and-reward program for those who contribute to a successful innovation, to encourage all employees to participate in the process.

Encouraging employees

Your employees must have the right attitude in order to come up with and develop innovations. An organization that operates a blame culture—in which mistakes are punished and instigators of new projects are made scapegoats when they fail—will discourage innovative thinking. On the other hand, a more open culture in which mistakes are treated as opportunities to learn and develop new strategies, will be more likely to encourage innovation. Discourage the attitude that current systems are perfectly fine, or "if it ain't broke, don't fix it," so that employees are constantly thinking of how their processes could be improved.

CASE STUDY

A culture of innovation

3M is often cited as an example of a consistently successful innovator that draws on what is clearly a highly innovative culture. 3M has around 50,000 products and yet is so confident in its ability to innovate that it sets the goal of deriving a third of its sales from products introduced in the past three years. Although it is famous for encouraging people to explore ideas not relevant to their main jobs, this is only one element of a complex culture. It also allows people to progress their ideas through stages of funding options, from seed money to greater resources, if the Board is convinced by the proposal. There is a deliberate attempt to create a sense of company history based on valuing those people who challenge the system, and a policy of encouraging "bootlegging" behavior—progressing innovation projects that might not have received official sanction.

Leading the way

Managers should also take a positive approach to creative ideas rather than expecting employees to just do as they are told. Sharing your vision of the company's future, and how innovation contributes to that vision, will encourage employee participation. Managers should support and communicate with workers throughout the company rather than remaining distant, so that new ideas can originate at any level.

CREATING AN INNOVATIVE CLIMATE

FACTORS	HOW IT INFLUENCES INNOVATIVE BEHAVIOR
Motivation	• People are driven to make their mark on the world and motivated by the degree to which they feel able to do so. • Staff can be highly motivated by recognition of their contribution from both peers and superiors.
Availability of slack resources	• People need resources to experiment with. • They need time and space to explore and create.
Leadership	• People need role models who exemplify key values and who support innovation in actions as well words. • They need leaders who consistently provide resources and motivation. • People value expressions of commitment at the strategic level.
Direction	• Innovation needs to be seen as strategically targeted and not just for the sake of it. • People will use measurement to drive improvement if they are motivated from within.
Self development	• It is important to help people continue to learn and acquire and use key skills.
Enabling tools and resources	• To contribute to the innovation task, people need training in systematic approaches to problem finding and solving.
Learning	• Learning helps people reflect on innovation experience. • It builds and extends understanding to guide action. • It encourages people to experiment. • Learning can be shared across the company.

Fostering creativity

Creativity not only generates the ideas that start an innovation, but also the means of fixing problems along the way. Scaling up, getting the bugs out of the system, and revising prototypes all require creative input. Understanding the creative process helps you to develop it in your organization.

IMPARTING THE SKILLS
Creative problem-solving is a skill like any other. Provide training to your employees, and make sure they obtain experience in finding and solving problems.

Thinking creatively

Creative problem-solving is a process psychologists have studied for years. There are four stages:
- **Recognition:** realizing you have a problem to solve.
- **Exploration:** examining different potential solutions. These may be obvious answers, or they may be tough, complex ideas that develop over time.
- **Insight:** the moment of connection, when an answer comes to you that you feel will resolve the problem.
- **Validation:** further examination of the idea as it is implemented to make sure it really is the solution.

In a business context, review and analysis should follow validation, to ensure the problem is solved. If not, the cycle repeats until an answer emerges.

Enhancing creativity

There are a number of proven strategies to enhance creativity in your organization. Building diversity will ensure that you have several perspectives available on a problem. Allow creative thinkers time and space to consider problems at length. Provide spaces for employees to develop their ideas—quiet rooms where individuals can concentrate, and group discussion areas where staff can gather to explore problems. And make sure that you give your staff a sense of freedom to try out different ideas, even if they don't always succeed.

Using creative tools

The good news is that there are many tools available to help you tackle the stages of the problem-solving cycle. These can be used by individuals, but most are more useful as part of a general meeting to enourage ideas.

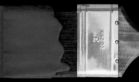

IDENTIFICATION
Fishbone (or "cause and effect") diagram—exploring the root causes of a problem and its contributing factors

REDEFINITION
Goal orientation—restating the problem to focus on what you are really trying to solve
Perspective—looking at the problem differently

EXPLORATION
Brainstorming—pooling ideas from a team
Radical ideas—encouraging wild thinking
Random link—forcing a random connection

SELECTION
Voting—a simple vote to choose the idea
Implement-ability matrix—plotting your ideas on a chart to compare the payoffs they offer

IMPLEMENTATION AND REVIEW
Measure and compare—reviewing an innovation project once it has been implemented to measure its success

Managing change

Implementing innovation means changing things, and many people are resistant to change, especially in their working conditions. It is important to understand the reasons for this resistance, and manage changes to minimize user uncertainty.

Understanding resistance

Not everyone is against change—some view it positively, while others resist any change at all. This could be due to several factors: they do not see the need for change, they are scared it will require them to do things of which they do not feel capable, they are worried about losing their jobs, they fear they will lose control over their work, they do not see what is in it for them, or they feel overloaded with what they already have to do.

COMMUNICATE ACTIVELY
Communication should be active, open, and timely (before the change occurs), and above all, two-way in practice.

Getting people on board

Change management is about understanding that uncertainty about change is natural, and dealing with the sources of that uncertainty. There are two types of resistance to change: the type you can tackle directly (by training people in new skills, for example), and the type that is emotional and maybe irrational. If someone feels their job is changing for the worse, that will shape the way they see the change, whether they are correct or not. You can address this only by creating a supportive climate where your employees can discuss and come to terms with their concerns.

BE SUPPORTIVE
Create an atmosphere in which individual concerns can be aired, and ideas within the organization used positively.

HAVE A CLEAR STRATEGY
Develop a vision and share it with the rest of the organization, to help employees feel ownership of it.

SET CLEAR TARGETS
Giving people clear goals and milestones will help them feel more confident about changes.

Changing tracks effectively

ENCOURAGE INVOLVEMENT
By allowing participation early in the change process, you ensure commitment to it and improvement in design.

INVEST IN TRAINING
Training is important for developing skills, continued improvement, and in creating a change-oriented organization.

Involving employees

Creativity comes as standard equipment with everyone who works in your organization. To paraphrase one manager, with every pair of hands there comes a free brain. The challenge lies in engaging this creativity—or how to tap into this resource to keep making innovation happen.

Involving over the long term

*CI—continuous improvement: a steady stream of incremental innovation. One of the most powerful engines for change in organizations is mobilizing the efforts of employees to deliver this.

An organization can choose to involve all employees in innovation (high involvement) or only a few (low involvement). The extent of involvement depends in part on whether the planned innovations are radical (high impact) or incremental (low impact). Either way, employees must feel motivated, empowered, and enabled to contribute if they are to help in innovation.

Once you have started the innovation process, the difficulty lies in keeping it going long enough to make a real difference. Many organizations start the process, have an initial surge of ideas and enthusiasm, and then see it gradually ebb away until there is little or no CI* activity. This isn't surprising—to change the way people think and behave on a long-term basis requires a strategic development program.

IN FOCUS... HIGH-INVOLVEMENT INNOVATION

High-involvement innovation has been around for a while. Denny's Shipyard in Dumbarton, Scotland, back in 1871 asked—and rewarded—workers for "any change by which work is rendered superior in quality or more economical in cost." It makes a big difference to firms like Toyota that do this on a systematic basis—it receives around two million suggestions a year from its workforce (Kawasaki Engineering, another high-involvement player, has a staggering seven million)—and it implements the majority of these.

Progressing in stages

Involvement in workplace innovation develops in five stages. You can use this model to identify the stage your organization has reached, and what needs to be done to progress toward higher involvement.

1 At level one innovation is random and occasional. People do help to solve problems, but there is no attempt to build on this, and organizations may actively restrict the opportunities for innovation to take place.

2 At level two an organization attempts to mobilize involvement. This needs a formal process for finding and solving problems in a structured and systematic way, and training employees to use it.

3 At level three high-involvement capability is coupled with the strategic goals of the organization, so that improvement activities of teams and individuals can be aligned. Strategy deployment, and monitoring and measuring are required for this.

4 At level four high involvement produces profit. Individuals and groups need to be empowered to innovate on their own initiative. This requires an understanding of, and commitment to, overall strategic objectives.

5 At level five the whole company is involved in experimenting with new ideas and improving processes, in sharing knowledge and creating the complete learning organization.

Involving customers

Everyone is creative—and that includes the end users of your innovation. Users are not simply passive consumers of new products or services; they will have plenty of ideas about how they would like to improve or change what they are using.

TIP

LISTEN TO COMPLAINTS
Pay attention to negative reactions from test users. If they reject your idea, it may not be worth pursuing.

Appreciating user involvement

An important theme in managing innovation is learning to work with users as co-creators of innovation ideas, for two good reasons. First, their ideas can help make a better innovation, and second, if you involve them they will buy into the idea. These users do not have to be limited to customers—the same applies to process innovation. Changes to the way people work can tap into their ideas about how the process should improve. Otherwise, they may find ways to resist the change. There are two ways of encouraging these ideas—appealing to specific users who are likely to contribute, and encouraging contributions from the entire user base.

Asking the best users

Focus groups identify users and their interests as an input to innovation design, and, later, as a sounding board. Prototyping and test marketing let you observe users' reactions to new ideas, and allow them to add their own. Lead-user methods help you identify early adopters among your user base, to help shape your idea while you develop it. Finally, communities of practice are small, often volunteer, groups of users that use innovative solutions on a continuing basis, such as the Linux community, music software groups like Propellerhead, and Apple's i-platform devices group.

Inviting ideas online

The Internet has made it possible for vast numbers of users to be contacted effortlessly, and for them to contribute ideas easily, widening your potential pool of ideas. Crowd-sourcing uses Web 2.0—the interactive, user-driven components of the Internet—to allow users to interact and provide their ideas to design and co-create products and services. Examples include Adidas, whose mi-Adidas platform lets you design your own shoes, and the Lego Factory website, where users can design their own Lego toys. Increasingly, companies like BMW, Kellogg, and Unilever are creating virtual innovation agencies, opening their doors to ideas from users by using the Internet to capture and review these ideas. Even simple arrangements like competitions and challenges can be a useful way of capturing user ideas focused on a particular challenge or target, especially if they are distributed over the Internet to encourage a large number of participants.

Networking for innovation

No person exists on their own, and no organization operates in isolation. Innovation has always been a multiplayer game, and in a world of "open innovation," where not all the smart people work for you, organizations are increasingly turning to networks to help them manage innovation.

TIP

COMBINE IDEAS

Once you and your innovators have been exposed to new ideas and concepts from other areas of your industry, or even other industries altogether, you can experiment to generate new concepts.

Maximizing resources

The benefits of innovation networks can be substantial. For small firms, the limiting factor is often that they are separated from developments in the wider market—they lack the overview of market intelligence a larger firm can access. Linking up in networks means they can tap into each other's resources, ideas, and knowledge. However, even larger firms are increasingly realizing how important a resource this can be, and adopting innovation network tactics accordingly. Innovation networks allow you to share resources and reduce potential risks of developing new products and processes. They give you diversity of perspectives, and access to knowledge sets and experience outside those in your organization.

ASK YOURSELF... HOW DEVELOPED IS YOUR CAPACITY FOR NETWORKING?

- Do I have links with a wide range of outside sources of knowledge—universities, research centers, and specialized agencies?
- Do I practice "open innovation" by using rich and widespread networks of contacts from whom I get a constant flow of challenging ideas?
- Does my approach to supply management permit "strategic dalliances"?
- Do I have contacts within the research and technology community?
- Do I recognize users as a source of new ideas and try to co-evolve new products and services with them?

UNDESTANDING TYPES OF INNOVATION NETWORK

NETWORK TYPE	EXAMPLES
Entrepreneur-based	Bringing different complementary resources together to help take an opportunity forward. This strategy is largely dependent on the entrepreneur's energy and enthusiasm in getting people interested in joining—and staying in—the network.
Communities of practice	Networks that involve players inside and across different organizations. They are bound together by a shared concern with a particular aspect or area of knowledge.
Spatial cluster	These form where key players in a given industry are situated in the same geographical area—Silicon Valley is a good example. Knowledge flow among and across the members of the network is helped by the geographical closeness and the ability of key players to meet and talk.
Sectoral network	These bring different players together because they share a common market sector or business model, and often have the purpose of shared innovation to preserve competitiveness.
New product or process development network	Networks that share knowledge and perspectives to create and market a new product or process concept across more than one organization.
Learning network	Working together across a sector or region to improve competitiveness through product, process, and service innovation.
New technology development network	Sharing and learning around newly emerging technologies to fully explore their potential—for example, the pioneering semiconductor research programs in the US and Japan that join resources and information from universities across the globe.
Emerging standards	Exploring and establishing standards around innovative technologies—for example, the Motion Picture Experts Group (MPEG) that works on audio and video compression standards for digital sound and video.
Supply chain learning	Developing and sharing innovative good practice and possibly shared product development across a value chain, such as between manufacture and distribution.

Networking and shared learning

*Shared learning—
*a process
of combining
knowledge
and experience
across teams or
organizations.*

The benefits of innovation networks don't happen by accident. Challenges to networking include: how to manage something you do not control; how to see system level effects and not self-interest; how to build shared risk-taking and avoid red tape; and how to avoid free riders who get benefits without contributing. The key issues in setting up a network are providing momentum for bringing the network together and clearly defining its purpose. The need for a network may be crisis-triggered or driven by a perception of opportunity. Third parties play key roles here: network brokers, gatekeepers, policy agents, and facilitators.

Networking also helps innovation by providing support for shared learning*, which alllows for the status quo to be challenged, and for assumptions to undergo critical reflection from different perspectives. Shared learning provides a wider perspective, prevents insular ideas, and brings in new concepts. Shared experimentation reduces the perceived and actual cost and risk of trying new things, and shared experiences can provide support and open new lines of exploration.

Managing the network

When the network is operational, you need some core operating processes on which all parties agree, such as:
• **Network boundary management:** how the membership of the network is defined and maintained.
• **Decision-making:** how (where, when, who) decisions get made at the network level.
• **Conflict resolution:** how conflicts are resolved.
• **Information processing:** how information flows among members and is managed.
• **Knowledge management:** how knowledge is created, shared, and used across the network.
• **Motivation:** how members are motivated to join and remain within the network.
• **Risk and benefit sharing:** how the risks and reward are allocated across members of the network.
• **Coordination:** how the operations of the network are integrated and coordinated.

Networks can be short-term and for a specific purpose, or they can continue for as long as members see it worthwhile—this may require periodic review and "retargeting" to keep motivation high.

AGREE ON THE TERMS

When setting up an innovation network, agree beforehand on how you plan to share potential profits, and losses, as well as how you will resolve conflicts.

Sharpening your skills

The capability to make innovation happen develops over time and through trial and error. To ensure your organization keeps improving its capacity for successful innovation, you need to diagnose how your organization manages the process.

Measuring efficiency

Innovation process measures include:
- Number of ideas generated at the start.
- Failure rates in the development process, and in the marketplace.
- Number or percentage of overruns on development time and budgets.
- Customer satisfaction measure—did the customers get what they wanted?
- Average time to market, compared with industry norms.
- Development time per completed innovation.
- Average lead time for the introduction of a process innovation.

Measuring innovation success

In addition to monitoring the efficiency of the process, it is also important to establish whether or not it is benefiting the organization as a whole. The first factors to measure are resources you devote to the process, such as time, money, training investment, strategic targeting, and overall guidance. These can be compared with outputs, such as the number of new products introduced, and profits derived from them; improvements in processes, calculated through customer satisfaction or efficiency surveys; comparisons with competitors; and overall business performance.

TIP

THINK LONG TERM
Review and audit even small-scale projects. This may not offer immediate benefits, but will make your organization better at innovation in the long run.

ASK YOURSELF... HOW GOOD ARE WE AT INNOVATION?

- Do we have a clear process for making innovation happen, and effective enabling mechanisms to support it as it progresses?
- Do we have a clear sense of shared strategic purpose, and do we use this to guide our innovative activities across the organization?
- Do we have a supportive organization whose structures and systems enable people to be creative and share and build on each other's ideas?
- Do we build and extend our networks for innovation into a rich and open innovation system?
- Do we actively try and learn to develop our capabilities for all of the above?

Measuring your own performance

In addition to organizational targets, it can be useful to monitor your own performance as a manager over the course of an innovation project. Make sure that you take time to review your projects so that you can improve your performance the next time. Learn from your mistakes, and capture what you have learned in a briefing document so that others in your organization can make use of it. Systematically compare your products and processes with those of other firms, and meet and share experiences with people in similar roles to yours. Look beyond your immediate organizational and geographical environment to ensure that you have the widest possible basis for new ideas, and encourage experimentation among your staff. Establish sets of measurable criteria for success to identify how and where you can improve your innovation management.

Index